W9-AGN-724

What If?.

What If an Asteroid Hit Earth?

Holly Cefrey

HIGH
interest
books

Children's Press®
A Division of Scholastic Inc.
New York / Toronto / London / Auckland / Sydney
Mexico City / New Delhi / Hong Kong
Danbury, Connecticut

Book Design: Michelle Innes and Michael DeLisio
Contributing Editors: Scott Waldman and Jennifer Silate
Photo Credits: Cover and p. 11 © Photodisc Space; pp. 4, 7, 15, 24, 33 © Photodisc
Spacescapes; pp. 5, 6, 13 © Gettyone FPG; p. 8 © Stapleton Collection/Corbis; pp. 9, 19,
21, 26 (top), 26 (bottom) © Photri Microstock; p.10 Illustration by Michael DeLisio; p. 14
© Reuters NewMedia Inc./Corbis; p. 16 © AP/Wide World Photos; p. 23 Illustration by
Michael DeLisio with images © Premium Stock/Corbis and Richard Cummins/Corbis;
p. 28 © Digital Vision Elements of Nature; p. 29 © Digital Vision Astronomy and Space;
pp. 31, 35, 36 © Roger Ressmeyer/Corbis; p. 32 © Corbis; p. 39 © Eyewire; p. 40 © Dennis
Degnan/Corbis

Library of Congress Cataloging-in-Publication Data

Cefrey, Holly.
What if an asteroid hit earth? / Holly Cefrey.
    p. cm. -- (What if?)
Includes index.
Summary: Discusses what might happen if an asteroid hit the Earth.
ISBN 0-516-23911-2 (lib. bdg.) -- ISBN 0-516-23475-7 (pbk.)
1. Asteroids--Collisions with Earth--Environmental aspects--Juvenile literature. 2.
Catastrophes (Geology)--Juvenile literature. [1. Asteroids. 2. Disasters.] I. Title. II. What
if? (Children's Press)

QB377 .C44 2002
363.3'49--dc21
                                                            2001037278

CONTENTS

INTRODUCTION

A massive black object speeds through space. It looks like a giant rock, with a jagged and dented surface. It spins around and around, making its journey through millions of miles of darkness. Just ahead are Earth and our moon.

This space rock is an asteroid. It has crossed the paths of other objects before. It is a large asteroid that has smashed smaller asteroids to bits. After each crash, pieces of the giant asteroid are left behind.

The asteroid is traveling at 55,000 miles (88,514 km) per hour. It's moving faster than anything made by humans. Should it hit Earth, it might kill several thousand people. It could also change life on our planet forever.

This asteroid is one of millions in our solar system. Our moon is scarred by past collisions with asteroids, as is Earth. According to the National Aeronautics and Space Administration (NASA), damaging asteroids strike Earth about once every 100,000 years.

An asteroid came dangerously close to hitting us

in 1996. It was about 1,760 feet (536 m) wide. It came within six hours of colliding with Earth. An asteroid of this size would have caused great damage. Scientists discovered it only four days before it almost hit Earth. Luckily, the asteroid just missed our planet.

What if this asteroid had hit Earth? Could an entire continent be wiped clean of life? This near-miss reminded many world leaders of the importance of watching for space objects. Efforts to protect people from an asteroid impact are being explored right now. Scientists hope to use technology to protect Earth.

CHAPTER ONE

Asteroid Basics

Asteroids are one kind of object that revolve around stars such as the sun. Objects such as planets, moons, and asteroids that revolve around the sun make up our solar system. The sun is the largest object in our solar system. It has the strongest gravity, or force of attraction. This force keeps the objects of our solar system revolving around it.

An orbit is the path of one object as it revolves around another object. Each object has its own special orbit. Orbits range in shape from near circles to ovals. Each object also has a different speed in its orbit. The orbits of different objects often overlap. Planets and asteroids orbit the sun while moons orbit planets.

Asteroids have to be at least 164 feet (50 m) in diameter to make it past Earth's atmosphere. Scientists believe that there are one million Near-Earth Asteroids that are larger than this.

The orbits of some asteroids place them in the direct path of Earth, the moon, and other planets. This is when impact can occur. An impact might have only minimal results. However, an impact could also mean the extinction of life on Earth.

THE MISSING PLANET

The Main Belt, or Asteroid Belt, contains more than 90 percent of the solar

William Herschel
(1738–1822)

In 1802, William Herschel, a British astronomer, first used the word *asteroid*. He used *asteroid* to describe objects that were not quite comets or planets but were definitely out there. The word is from the Greek language and means "starlike."

Herschel is known for building the largest telescope of his time. He also accidentally discovered Uranus. Herschel first thought Uranus was a comet. Later the object was determined to be a planet.

system's asteroids. The Main Belt is located between the orbits of Jupiter and Mars.

Scientists also refer to asteroids in the Main Belt

as minor planets. According to NASA, more than ten thousand known minor planets are in the belt. Millions more have yet to be named and charted.

Space materials, including asteroids, slowly grouped together to form planets. It took over a million years for the planets to form. Scientists believe that the Main Belt was created while the solar system was forming. This was about 4.6 billion years ago.

Scientists believe that the Main Belt is made up of the remains of a planet that could not form near Jupiter. Jupiter is the largest planet of our solar system.

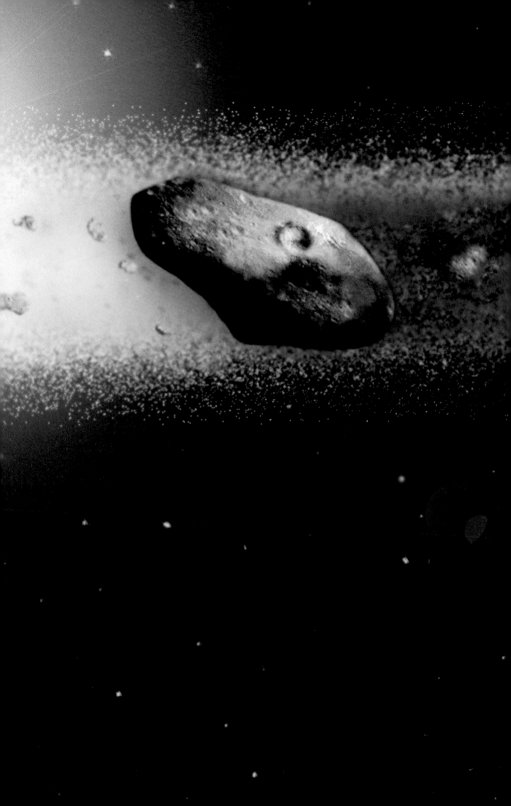

It's 320 times larger than Earth. Jupiter's gravity may have caused nearby asteroids to crash into each other at high speeds. These collisions forced the asteroids apart instead of allowing them to group together and form a planet. Those asteroids formed the Main Belt.

SPACE STUFF

Asteroids aren't the only objects that Earth encounters during its orbit. Earth also crosses paths with comets, meteoroids, meteors, and meteorites.

Comets—small, irregularly-shaped objects made of ice and dust

Meteoroids—pieces of rock and dust that come from asteroids, comets, or other planets

Meteor—a streak of light across the sky ("shooting star"), which is a meteoroid being burned up as it enters our atmosphere

Meteorites—meteoroids that reach Earth's surface without being burned up

Many asteroids are shaped like potatoes. They are covered with craters, caused by space objects crashing into them.

ASTEROID BREAKDOWN

Asteroids may be made of rock, metal, or a combination of both. They can be different colors. Asteroids range in shape and size. They can be as small as a pebble. They can also be as large as the state of Texas. Small asteroids are more common than large ones. Scientists believe that most large asteroids collide with objects in space. This breaks them into smaller asteroids.

When asteroids crash into other objects, the results may be:

- **Craters**—bowl-shaped dents on the surface of an object. Craters are made when small asteroids strike larger objects. The crater will appear on the larger object. The small asteroid usually crumbles.
- **Grouping of asteroid pieces**—An asteroid can strike another asteroid and cause it to break into pieces. The pieces stay together and orbit as one ball.
- **Scattering of asteroid pieces**—After an asteroid breaks into pieces, the pieces scatter into separate orbits.

Asteroids come in many sizes. The largest known asteroid is named Ceres. It is 578 miles (933 km) in diameter.

There is evidence of both grouped and scattered crashes in the Main Belt. The surfaces of the earth, moon, and other planets are covered with craters. The craters cause scientists to wonder when the next asteroid will strike. They also want to know what will happen when it does.

CHAPTER TWO

Global Ground Zero

Asteroid impacts on Earth date back to its beginning. More than 150 craters are on Earth's surface. Some of these craters are very old and some are fairly recent. Asteroids, comets, and meteorites are responsible for the craters.

The Chicxulub Crater lies off the coastline of Mexico. It was made sixty-five million years ago. The crater is about 124 miles (200 km) wide. Some scientists believe that an asteroid the size of a mountain struck Earth there. Scientists believe the effects of this impact could have killed off the dinosaurs.

A 100-foot-wide (30 m) asteroid struck Earth fifty thousand years ago. It left a crater in Arizona that is

If an asteroid does make it through Earth's atmosphere, it will most likely hit an ocean. This is because almost three-fourths of the Earth is covered with water.

This photo was taken in Tunguska, Russia, forty-five years after the asteroid explosion.

almost 1 mile (1.6 km) wide. In February 1947, 25 tons (22,680 kg) of space rock fell on the Sikhote-Alin Mountains in Siberia. The impact of these rocks left craters as wide as 85 feet (137 km).

Asteroids can still be damaging to Earth even if they don't reach the surface. In June 1908, an asteroid exploded 3 to 5 miles (4.8 to 8 km) above Earth's surface. As this asteroid moved through Earth's atmosphere, it became heated due to friction. This heat caused the asteroid to explode over the Tunguska River region in Siberia. Fortunately, few people were living in the area. Two people were killed. The blast flattened trees in an 18-mile (29 km) radius and killed thousands of reindeer. The explosion was heard more than 620 miles (998 km) away.

ASTEROIDS ABOUND

Agencies such as NASA keep track of asteroid movement. NASA researchers give names to the asteroids and watch their orbits. More than ten thousand asteroids have been named and tracked. Researchers watch asteroids so they can be aware of any that could possibly collide with Earth.

Many of the known asteroids are close to Earth. These asteroids are called Near-Earth Asteroids, or NEAs. NEAs are asteroids with orbits that bring them within 121 million miles (193 million km) of Earth. According to NASA, there are millions of NEAs. NEAs larger than 1 mile wide (1.6 km) are capable of causing major damage to Earth.

About one thousand NEAs are a half-mile (.8 km) wide or more. The largest NEAs are 15 miles (24 km) wide. It's believed that the asteroid responsible for the extinction of the dinosaurs was about 9 miles (14 km) wide. It struck Earth with 100 million megatons of power. That's about the power of more than four million nuclear bombs going off at once.

STRIKING EARTH

Scientists see three possible scenarios if the orbit of an asteroid of this size puts it in the path of Earth. One, the asteroid is discovered in time and scientists can try to change its orbit. Two, the asteroid is noticed too late to prevent an impact. And three, an asteroid hits Earth without any warning at all. In the last two scenarios, people on Earth would have no time to prepare themselves.

Sudden Impact

Many small objects that enter Earth's atmosphere burn up before reaching the surface. However, objects that are too large to burn up can make it through the

An asteroid 9 miles (14 km) wide entering Earth's atmosphere would create an explosion with 250,000 times the power of an eruption of a large volcano.

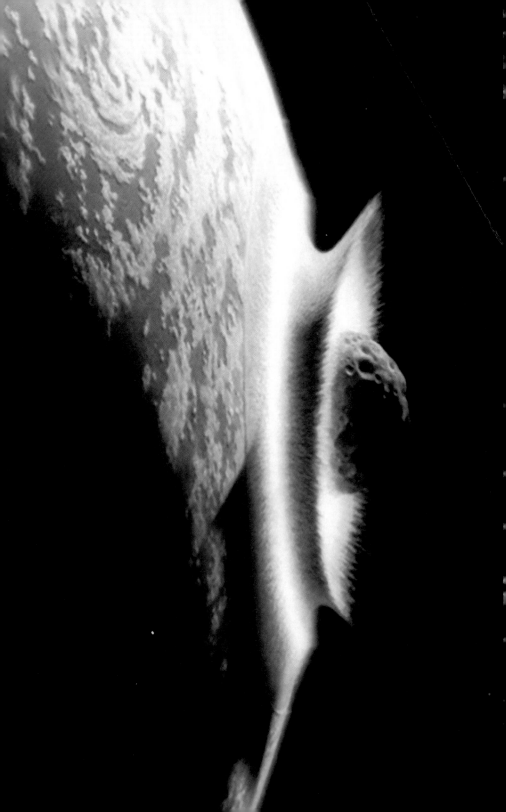

atmosphere. They maintain their speed and power as they drop to the surface.

The protective layers of Earth's atmosphere are no match for a huge asteroid. In less than a second, the asteroid heats the air it passes through to 50,000°F (27,760°C). The air changes to a deadly gas. The gas looks like white clouds reaching toward the sky.

Water makes up over 70 percent of Earth's surface. Chances are good that asteroids would strike water instead of land. As the asteroid plunges into the ocean, the water temperature immediately rises to 100,000°F (55,538°C). Nearby marine life is boiled and destroyed within seconds.

Ground Zero

The asteroid strikes the ocean floor. One hundred million megatons of power are released into Earth. This point of impact is called ground zero. Within seconds, the whole planet starts shaking from this tremendous force.

There is a deafening sound and a blinding light. A mixture of water (over 100 billion trillion gallons),

The impact of a huge asteroid would cause tsunamis to flood most of the land on Earth.

asteroid bits, and ocean bedrock shoots out from ground zero. It travels at 25,000 miles (40,000 km) per hour.

An immense fireball forms from the steam and melting rock. This fireball lashes out 1,000 miles (1,600 km) from ground zero. The fireball burns everything it touches down to a bare rock surface.

The asteroid leaves a hole in the ocean floor that is 200 miles (322 km) wide. It is 10 miles (16 km) deep.

The hole fills up with boiling water and rocks until a crater remains. Its final size will be about 60 miles (97 km) wide. It will be about 1,760 feet (536 m) deep. Above the water, Earth is about to suffer a terrible fate.

Deadly Global Storms

The air is heated to about 3,000°F (1,649°C). It produces winds as strong as a hurricane. The winds ravage the surface of Earth for the next 20 hours.

The shaking of the planet produces ocean waves. The waves grow into tsunamis as high as the Rocky Mountains. These tsunamis travel more than 400 miles (644 km) per hour. They wash over the land. The devastating force of the waves drowns thousands of people and other land animals.

More lasting damage is about to begin. Within hours and days of impact, sunlight is blocked from Earth. The damage resulting from this can last for millions of years after the impact.

The impact of a large asteroid hitting an ocean would cause sea levels to rise.

CHAPTER THREE

The Lasting Darkness

Trillions of tiny rock particles fly back toward the sky upon impact. The particles reach our ozone layer within seconds. The particles spread out and form clouds when they reach the upper part of our atmosphere. No sunlight passes through these clouds. Earth is in complete darkness.

The air 40 miles (64 km) above the surface is heated to 1,800°F (982°C). Earth's surface temperature rises to 600°F (316°C) for several hours. The high temperature destroys any life that is unable to shield itself. Anything that can burn instantly bursts into flames.

Blanket of Darkness

Soot from the burning earth rises toward the darkening sky. Soon the air turns to smog that is over 17 miles (27 km) thick. The smog combines with the spreading particles and blankets Earth in less than 24 hours.

The darkness caused by smog and particles doesn't go away—it lasts several months or years. Without the sunlight, most life cannot exist. Our air and water becomes poisonous and deadly.

Acid Rain

Rain begins to fall. The rain contains acids capable of destroying life. The acid rain also brings out poisonous metals from rocks and soil. The rain washes the poisons into rivers, ponds, and streams. They kill any remaining marine life.

Soon Earth grows cold because of the lack of sunlight. Within ten days, the planet experiences temperatures colder than those of Arctic winters. Scientists call this effect "impact winter."

Before Acid Rain

After Acid Rain

This is what acid rain did to a forest in Vermont over a twenty-year period. The effects of acid rain caused by an asteroid impact would be much worse.

Impact Winter

The impact winter lasts years. The entire globe experiences below-freezing temperatures. Snow falls and forms a 20-foot-thick (6 m) layer. However, this isn't normal snow because it contains the same acids as the rain.

A very small number of creatures may still be alive. Those that do survive are capable of living in harsh temperatures and without food. Everything else freezes or starves to death.

Eventually the smog begins to clear. Sunlight reaches Earth again. Earth's atmosphere is still not balanced, though. It traps the sun's heat instead of releasing it. A steamy hot climate replaces the impact winter around the globe. This may last for a few million years.

Earth Anew

New life returned to Earth after the asteroid impact sixty-five million years ago. It took millions of years for impact damage to disappear. It's believed that new life started forming in these years.

If an asteroid struck Earth again, new creatures would probably appear. Despite the devastating damage, Earth would most likely return to being a living planet.

Near-Earth Asteroid Groups

There are three different groups of known NEAs that come near Earth or Earth's orbit. The groups are not part of the Main Belt. The asteroid groups make their own orbit around the sun.

- **Apollo Group**—follows an orbit that takes it directly across Earth's path

- **Amor Group**—follows an orbit that takes it between the orbits of Earth and Mars

- **Aten Group**—follows an orbit that takes it between the orbits of Earth and Venus

After an asteroid impact, will Earth return to being a living planet?

IMPACT–A REAL THREAT?

Presently, there are over 250 named and charted NEAs. Out of this number, none are on a collision course with Earth. More than half of the larger NEAs (a half-mile [.8 km] wide or more) have also been discovered. None of these are expected to crash into Earth. However, NASA estimates that there are many more large NEAs yet to be discovered. There is no way of predicting if any of these will strike Earth until they are discovered.

The best way to predict an impact is to constantly search space for asteroids. Many scientific organizations across the globe are doing just that. Hopefully, scientists will be able to use technology to prevent a global impact.

Scientists take pictures of asteroids and other space objects using telescopes and spacecrafts.

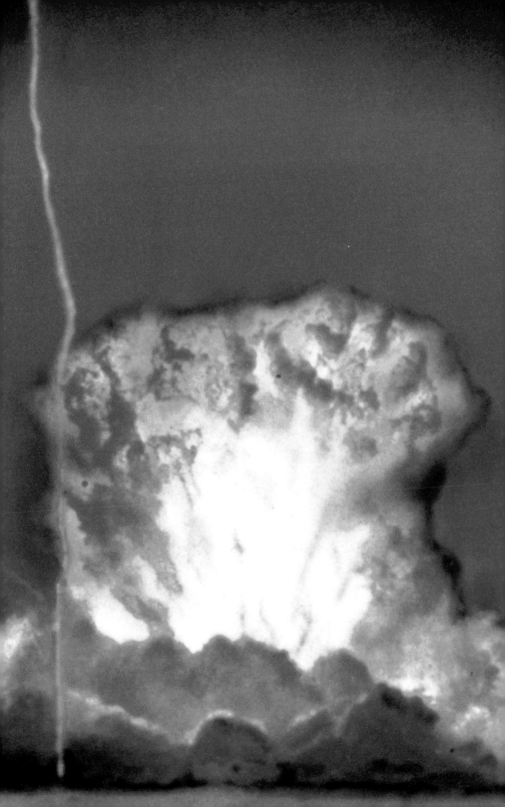

CHAPTER FOUR

Protecting Our Planet

Nuclear bombs could be used to destroy an asteroid on a collision course toward Earth. A rocket carrying a nuclear bomb could be fired at the asteroid. The explosion of the bomb would shatter the asteroid into smaller pieces. A bomb could also be used to knock the asteroid out of its orbit if it's too large to destroy.

Another solution would be to land rocket engines on the asteroid. Firing these rocket engines could direct the asteroid off its course.

SEARCHING THE SKIES

Astronomers are scientists who study space. In addition to NEAs, they study comets, meteors, and other space objects. These objects are called NEOs,

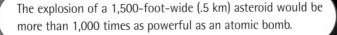

The explosion of a 1,500-foot-wide (.5 km) asteroid would be more than 1,000 times as powerful as an atomic bomb.

or Near-Earth Objects. There are organized teams of scientists around the world who search for NEAs and NEOs.

However, there are many objects in space. More teams of "sky-watchers" are needed to completely search space. With more people involved, it's less likely that an NEA or NEO would remain unnoticed.

Scientists and astronomers aren't the only people who watch the sky. The world is filled with amateur, or hobbyist, astronomers. They locate, study, and report space objects to government space programs. Amateur astronomers play a valuable role in our knowledge of NEAs and NEOs.

SPACE WATCH PROGRAMS

NASA plays an important role in establishing, funding, and operating programs that research asteroids. NASA also works with other organizations and governments in asteroid research.

An organized study of asteroid movement is called a survey. Surveys are carried out on the ground

Observatories around the world are looking for NEAs and NEOs.

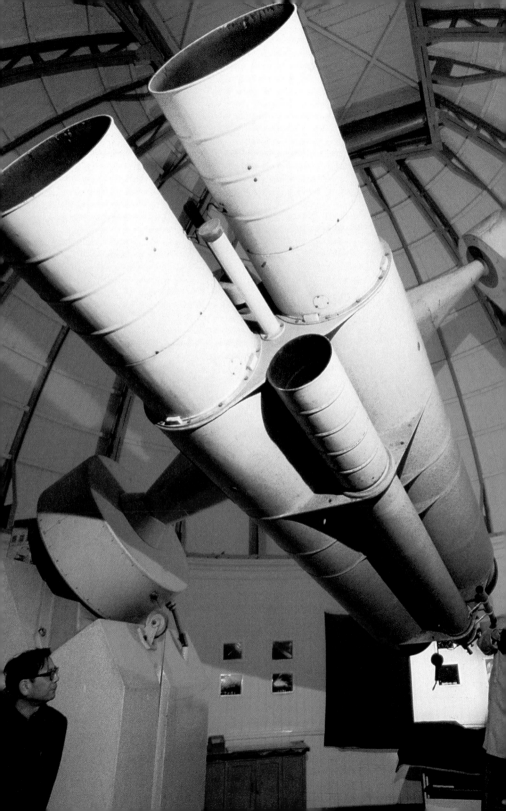

through the use of telescopes. They are carried out in space through the use of spacecrafts.

Surveys

Spaceguard was formed in an effort to link all the survey data from different programs around the world. Spaceguard is an international agency that was started in Rome in 1996. Surveys have been carried out in China, France, Japan, and the United States. The following surveys were carried out in the United States.

- **LINEAR** (Lincoln Near-Earth Asteroid Research): Carried out by NASA and the U.S. Air Force in New Mexico

- **LONEOS** (Lowell Observatory Near-Earth Object Survey): Supported by NASA in Arizona

- **NEAT** (Near-Earth Asteroid Tracking): Carried out by NASA and the U.S. Air Force in California and Hawaii

- **Spacewatch**: Carried out by NASA in Arizona and supported by private grants

Scientists use powerful telescopes to check the sky for asteroids and other space objects.

Space Surveys

One of the most exciting moments in space survey occurred on February 12, 2001 with the NEAR Shoemaker spacecraft. The NEAR (Near-Earth Asteroid Rendezvous) spacecraft actually landed on an asteroid.

This asteroid is named 433 Eros. Eros is a gigantic asteroid. Its dimensions are 20.5 by 8 by 8 miles (33 by 13 by 13 km). The asteroid was over 160 million miles (257 million km) from Earth when NEAR landed.

The spacecraft orbited Eros for a year before landing gracefully on its surface. NEAR was able to send back information about the asteroid. NEAR's pictures of Eros showed tiny rocks on its surface. There are also broken boulders and dust-filled craters. Scientists will get another good look at Eros in January 2012. Its orbit will bring it only 16.6 million miles (26.7 million km) from Earth.

You Can Join the Team!

Amateur astronomers search space by using telescopes. If you don't have a telescope, you can help to

You can see stars, planets, and even galaxies through a telescope in your own backyard!

research space. There are sites on the Internet that allow you to use their data to research space.

An example of an organization with such a site is the Hubble Deep Field Academy of the Space Telescope Science Institute. Its site is designed for teachers, students, and others who are interested in space study. The Web addresses are at the back of this book.

Many space enthusiasts feel that our space agencies do not receive enough money from the government. With more funding, the agencies would have more resources to study space. You can write letters to your local government officials, urging them to support space research programs. Public support often encourages the government to find funds for programs.

Computers open up a world of possibilities for space research.

NEW WORDS

asteroid a space rock that orbits the sun; most are located in the Main Belt

astronomers scientists who study space and space objects

comets small, irregularly-shaped objects made of ice and dust

crater a pit created by the impact of two objects colliding

friction a force between two objects that creates heat

gravity a force of attraction between two objects

ground zero the point of impact between two objects

impact winter the extreme cold climate that would occur after debris from an asteroid blocks sunlight and heat

Main Belt an area between Mars and Jupiter where asteroids are grouped; also called the Asteroid Belt

megatons equal to one million tons of TNT each

meteor a streak of light across the sky ("shooting star"), which is a meteoroid being burned up in Earth's atmosphere

meteorites meteoroids that reach Earth's surface without being burned up

meteoroids pieces of rock and dust that come from comets, asteroids, or other planets

orbit the path of an object as it revolves around another object

solar system the sun and all of the space objects that orbit it

tsunamis huge ocean waves

FOR FURTHER READING

Becklake, Sue. *Space: Stars, Planets, and Spacecraft.* New York: DK Publishing, 1998.

Kerrod, Robin. *Astronomy.* New York: Lorenz Books, 1996.

Lippincott, Kristen. *Eyewitness: Astronomy.* New York: DK Publishing, 2000.

Pratt Nicolson, Cynthia. *Exploring Space.* Toronto, Canada: Kids Can Press, 2000.

Pearce, Q.L. *Strange Science—Outer Space.* New York: Tor Books, 1999.

RESOURCES

Organizations

Students for the Exploration and Development of Space (SEDS)
MIT Room W20-445
77 Massachusetts Avenue
Cambridge, MA 02139-4307
(888) 321-SEDS
http://www.seds.org/seds

NASA Headquarters Information Center
Washington, DC 20546-0001
(202) 358-0000
Fax: (202) 358-3251
http://www.nasa.gov

RESOURCES

Web Sites

Hubble Deep Field Academy
http://amazing-space.stsci.edu/hdf-top-level.html
Learn about the Hubble Space Telescope, comets, and other space objects on this site.

Lincoln Laboratory—MIT
http://www.ll.mit.edu
On this Web site, you can see pictures from outer space and learn about the Lincoln Laboratory.

NEAT (Near-Earth Asteroid Tracking)
http://neat.jpl.nasa.gov
This site has news about, and tracks the orbit of NEAs.

SpaceDaily
http://www.spacedaily.com
Get up-to-date space news on this informative Web site.

INDEX

INDEX

About the Author
Holly Cefrey is a freelance writer and researcher.